Jump and Shout

CHEERLEADING SKILLS

TRACY NELSON MAURER

Rourke
Publishing LLC
Vero Beach, Florida 32964

Project Assistance courtesy of Jennifer Tell, Dance and Cheer Factory, Forest Lake, Minnesota.

The author also extends appreciation to Mike Maurer, Kendall and Lois Nelson, the Rourke team, Nancy Zadow, and the University of Minnesota Alumni Association.

Photo Credits: Cover, Title, pg 35 ©PHOTOSPORT.COM
pgs 37, 38, 40, 41, 42 ©Paul Martinez/PHOTOSPORT.COM
pgs 4, 9, 43 ©Peter Schlitt/PHOTOSPORT.COM
pgs 6, 7, 14, 16, 19, 20, 22, 23, 24, 25, 26, 27, 29, 30, 32, 33, 44 ©PIR

Editor: Frank Sloan

Cover and page design: Nicola Stratford

Notice: This book contains information that is true, complete, and accurate to the best of our knowledge. However, the author and Rourke Publishing LLC offer all recommendations and suggestions without any guarantees and disclaim all liability incurred in connection with the use of this information.

Safety first! Activities appearing or described in this publication may be dangerous. Always work with a trained coach and spotters when learning new cheerleading skills.

Library of Congress Cataloging-in-Publication Data

Library of Congress Cataloging-in-Publication Data

Maurer, Tracy, 1965-
  Cheerleading skills / Tracy Nelson Maurer.
    p. cm. -- (Jump and shout)
  Summary: "Cheerleaders blend amazing athletic skills and spirited talent to perform breathtaking stunts. They work hard to boost school pride and win over judges at stiff competitions. Coaches expect teamwork, dedication, good grades, and healthy attitudes"--Provided by publisher.
  Includes bibliographical references and index.
  ISBN 1-59515-500-7 (hardcover : alk. paper)
  1. Cheerleading--Juvenile literature. I. Title. II. Series.
LB3635.M28 2006
791.6'4--dc22

                    2005012630

Printed in the USA

cg/cg

Rourke Publishing
1-800-394-7055
www.rourkepublishing.com
sales@rourkepublishing.com
Post Office Box 3328, Vero Beach, FL 32964

TABLE OF CONTENTS

Remember to face the crowd and keep smiling.

Chapter 1

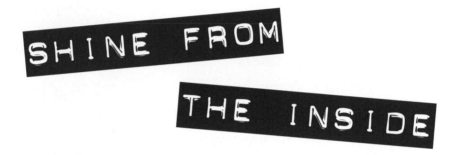

SHINE FROM THE INSIDE

Cheerleaders look like fun people to know. They're confident. They have positive attitudes. They're often good at sports, and they're often "good sports" too, even when their team loses.

Did you notice? Not one of these characteristics has anything to do with their looks.

Maybe cheerleaders are pretty. Maybe not. Coaches look for cheerleaders whose personalities shine from the inside out.

So, if beauty is not required for cheerleading, then what is?

Projection is a major requirement. Projection is the way you use your face, eye contact, body movements, and voice to communicate to the crowd. Coaches also want to see rhythm, coordination, flexibility, strength, and **endurance**. Of course, newbies must master basic cheerleading skills, such as hand clasps and jumps, too.

Coaches host tryouts to see all the candidates in action. Wannabes often practice with the existing team. Practice time might be limited to an hour before the tryouts or it might be scheduled over several weeks.

Don't miss the practice opportunity! It's your best chance to learn what the coach expects and to show the coach that you're serious about joining the team.

A big smile and good eye contact will keep the fans engaged.

Stand straight with good form, and you will look confident.

Skill Drill: Smile!

Smiling is a major projection skill. A cheerleader smiles in the rain. She smiles when the team loses. She smiles when she really wants to be at the biology class party instead. During a game, her hardworking smile lights up her face. The crowd smiles back.

Smiling makes you feel good every time you practice. Try it the next time you're feeling down or crabby. Smile, smile, smile.

Do you wear braces? Nobody can see them from the crowd. Ditto crooked teeth, teeth with spaces between them, or teeth with less than Cameron Diaz perfection.

Walk with your head up, shoulders back, and eyes looking directly at everyone you meet. Show that you can handle yourself with grace under pressure. When you goof up, don't melt down. Keep going. Keep smiling. That's what the crowd and the coaches want to see.

Mirror Magic

Practice in front of a mirror. Check your smile while you cheer. Are your shoulders back? What does your body language say? Watching yourself in the mirror also helps to improve your eye contact with the crowd.

Voice Projection

Can you project your voice clearly and loudly to crowds up to 500 feet (152 meters) away?

Muscles control your voice, just like muscles control your legs. You probably didn't do the splits the first time, right? To master your voice projection, you need to train your muscles to push more air from your lungs over your vocal cords.

"Vocal cords" politely describe two folds of **mucous membrane**. They look like two slimy window shades forming a V-shaped opening. The V closes when you swallow. No choking allowed.

Remember to project your voice up and out.

When the V opens, air coming from the lungs can rattle the two window shades together. The **vibration** is your voice, fine-tuned into words by your teeth, tongue, and lips.

Try this experiment. Whisper, *"Whispering does not project my voice."*

When you whisper, you hold your vocal cords still. Air flows through the V, but the vocal cords can't vibrate. So, no sound.

Yelling from your throat uses a wimpy air supply. And it hurts. Train your **diaphragm**, that plunger-type muscle just below your lungs, to amp up your volume. It moves down and creates a vacuum that sucks air deeply into your lungs. Stand up straight for more suction. Squeeze your upper stomach muscles, or **abs**, when you exhale.

Breath Test

Are you breathing correctly? Inhale deeply. Place one hand lightly on your chest and yell. Does your chest rumble? Try it with your hand on your throat. If you feel the sound moving through your throat, squeeze those abs tighter when you exhale.

Sounds Right

Vocal cords act like guitar strings. The tighter they are, the higher they sound. That's your pitch. Squeals, screams, and other high-pitched sounds do not reach as far as lower pitches. Using a high-pitched voice tenses your vocal cords and tweaks your listeners. Stay on the lower end of your natural pitch.

Volume and pitch deliver your voice to the crowd. But to understand your cheers, the fans need you to clearly **enunciate** each word, especially the word endings. Do you want the team to FIGH or FIGHT? Really watch those "T" and "D" sounds.

Separate the words and emphasize each syllable. At the end of the cheer, stretch out the last word. The audience knows this is its cue to start clapping.

No Lame Hoarses

You sound hoarse or raspy when your vocal cords can't vibrate properly. If your voice becomes hoarse often or it stays hoarse for more than a week, talk to your doctor.

Protect your voice.

* Don't hang out in smoky rooms (duh) and don't smoke (double duh).
* Stand up straight to stretch the vocal cords and allow full air flow.
* Drink lots of water every day to keep those mucous membranes moist and slimy.
* Don't forget to stand up straight.
* Soothe tired vocal cords with lukewarm water, tea, or juice.
* Don't drink milk or eat dairy foods before you perform; a-hem: phlegm. Eck.
* Warm up your vocal cords before cheering by singing in an easy range.
* Relax your neck and shoulder muscles.
* Try not to clear your throat over and over again.
* Posture, posture, posture.
* Sleep with a humidifier if your throat feels dry.
* Remember to stand up straight!

Chapter 2

THREE CHEERS

FOR SAFETY

Before cheerleaders learn basic positions, they learn about safety. Yes, you can get hurt cheerleading. Sprained ankles top the list. Head and neck injuries don't happen very often these days, but when they do—they're not pretty. A head-first crash landing can break your neck or crack your skull. Either way, you would have a good chance of **paralysis** and even death.

Don't try difficult moves without help from a well-trained coach. Lack of supervision + lack of experience = double trouble.

Cheerleading is a physical activity, and accidents can happen even when safety procedures are followed.

Overall, cheerleading is a relatively safe activity. Cheerleaders spend less time in the emergency room than basketball or football players (whose "seasons" are about six months shorter than most cheerleaders' seasons). It's up to you to help keep those injury statistics low.

How Do You Spell Safety?

Think safety when you practice, when you go to cheerleading camp, and when you perform. Here's an old-school spelling cheer to remember SAFETY first.

Give me an S!
Stunt only after you understand the moves and an experienced coach helps you.

Give me an A!
Ask your coach for warm-up and stretching exercises before and after you practice and perform.

Give me an F!
Find fabrics that aren't slippery for practice outfits and performance uniforms.

Give me an E!
Empty your mouth: no gum, candy, or other food.

Give me a T!
Take off all jewelry, tie up your hair, and tuck in your shirt.

Give me a Y!
Yell your counts during practices—clear communication prevents injuries.

What does it spell? SAFETY, SAFETY, SAFETY!

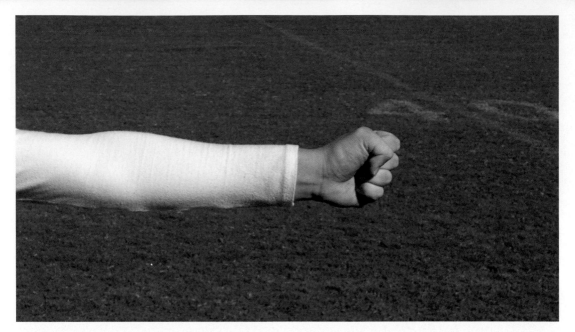

Your thumb goes on the outside when forming a basic fist.

The bucket fist position

Chapter 3

POSITIONS, EVERYONE!

Every team creates unique cheers and special moves. But they start with the same basic positions that all cheerleaders learn. Many coaches expect you to show some of these skills at tryouts.

Fists First

Your hands form exclamation points for your body language. They add emphasis to cheers. Every hand movement should be sharp and clean. Wishy-washy **gestures** look like you're waving dead fish.

Basic Fist

Squeeze your fingers together under your thumb, not around your thumb. Tucking in your thumb is like sticking it into a nutcracker. (See top picture, page 16.)

Bucket

Imagine you're holding a bucket. Your thumb is on the bottom of the fist and your knuckles point upward. (See bottom picture, page 16.)

Knocker

This is like the bucket position, except the knocker thumb faces forward. It looks like you're about to knock on a door.

Candlestick

Make a fist "candle" with the knuckles turned to the side. Your thumb points ahead, pressing down on the fist (snuffing out the flame).

Dagger

Make a fist with the little finger facing out to the crowd and knuckles pointing upward, as if you've raised a dagger in battle.

Blade

Use a flat, open hand with straight fingers. Your thumb faces forward and glued to the point finger. Don't let it hang out where it can break.

The candlestick fist position

The blade position

A cheerleader demonstrates the blade clap.

Hand Movements

Clap

You started clapping as a baby. It's time to perfect it. Cup your hands to amp up the volume. Slap your right-hand fingers between the left-hand thumb and pointer finger, and let your thumbs crisscross. Your hands meet under your chin and about 4 inches (10 cm) away from your body. Keep your elbows locked by your ribs. Just your lower arms move. Hold the same position without noise for hand clasps.

Blade Clap

Using the blade hand position, make sure your hands meet under your chin and about 4 inches (10 cm) away from your body. Crack your hands together with the same crisp movement as the basic clap.

Sparkles

Spread out your fingers and wiggle your wrists. Your hands become visual **pompons**.

Arm Positions

Spectators far away can't see your hands as well as they can see your arms. Use your arms to express your body language. Always shift your arm positions with strong and snappy movements to tell the crowd that you're excited—and they should be too!

Teams often make up their own arm positions, but some positions are the same everywhere. Your coach might use a variety of hand positions with each arm position. Keep your wrists straight for most positions.

Arms in the hips position

Hips

Plant a fist on each hip with bent elbows pointed out to the sides like little wings.

High V

Raise your straight arms and tight fists in the air, just ahead of your face (look for them in your **peripheral** vision). For polish, turn your fists outward so your thumbnails face the crowd.

Low V

Reach down with straight arms, again just ahead of your body. Turn your fists so the thumbnails face inward.

The high-V position is used when standing on the ground or in a flyer position.

T-Position

Make the letter T with your body, pointing your straight arms out on each side. They should be **parallel** to the ground and just a bit in front of you. Keep your fists tight and point your thumbnails to the ground.

Cheerleaders practice the T position.

Broken T

Make a T, but bend your elbows with your fists tucked by your shoulders. Point your thumbnails at your armpits.

Arms in the broken-T position

Touchdown

Pretend you're a football referee! Raise your straight arms in the air like goalposts. Keep them next to your head and turn your thumbnails in so they point at each other.

Low Touchdown

Do an upside-down touchdown. Reach downward with arms straight and parallel. Thumbnails point inward.

High Punch

This is useful for showing "We're Number One!" Raise your straight right arm next to your right ear. The thumbnail faces inward. Put your left fist on your left hip.

High punch

Foot Steps

Cheerleading guys do a lot of lifting and tossing that require solid foot or leg positions. Guys don't move as much as the gals. Guys should learn all of the basic positions anyway to help the entire squad master new cheers faster.

Feet Together / Apart

Straight legs need planted feet. *Together* means evenly side by side, not one foot ahead or behind the other. *Feet apart* should be slightly wider than shoulder width. Cheer routines often start and end with either of these positions.

Feet together

Feet apart

Clean Position

The clean position is a common starting and ending position for cheers. Point your arms down straight and hold your hands in the blade position by your thighs with your feet together.

Kneel

Guys kneel more often than gals do. One knee is on the ground and the other leg bends 90° at the knee, like a prince proposing.

Front Lunge

Step forward and bend your front leg. Gals pop up on your toes (guys keep their front foot flat). Keep the back leg straight and foot flat.

Back Lunge

Similar to a front lunge, step forward and bend your front leg (same deal on the toes). Your hips face forward as you shift your weight to the straight back leg.

Stag

Raise one bent knee hip-high and tuck that foot under your seat with the toes pointing down. Balance on the other foot.

Front lunge

High Kick

Popular in dance moves, kicks also show up in cheers. Keep your back straight the entire time. Plant one foot firmly. Snap up your other leg, pointing your toes and holding the kicking leg straight. Stretching exercises will boost your flexibility, strength, and balance for faster and higher kicks.

Hit the Crowd

Hold your last motion for a few seconds at the end of a cheer. This adds impact and tells fans to applaud. Then "hit the crowd" by making eye contact with several people as you jump, clap, or kick a few more times to encourage the fans to join you.

Chapter 4

JUMPS AND STUNTS

Cheerleading started at a University of Minnesota football game in 1889 without any breathtaking jumps or stunts. Loud voices and oodles of **enthusiasm** worked fine for Johnny Campbell and his buddies then. After female students were finally allowed to join the school's pep squad, the U of MN ladies introduced the first tumbling moves to cheerleading in the 1920s.

Over time, cheerleading has added more and more exciting elements. Today's fans expect cheerleaders to perform spectacular jumps and stunts.

Ready, Six, Seven, Eight

Like dancers, cheerleaders use a counting system to time their moves. An eight-count beat works well for practicing jumps. The coach says, "Ready, six, seven, eight…" The squad picks it up from there, counting out loud from one to eight and moving on each of those eight beats.

For a jump, the series of eight-count movements breaks into three parts: the set-up or prep, the jump, and the landing.

Jumps use arm positions that help lift your body into the air. Your arms swing down from a high position (like tightening up a spring) and then quickly snap upward again (like releasing a spring). This circular **momentum** adds height to the jump.

Your main power comes from your legs, especially quadriceps (thighs). Bending at the knees coils your body's energy. As you leap, the large thigh muscles powerfully release the energy and propel you upward.

When you're airborne, hit the jump position. The landing comes next—and quickly! For a clean and soft landing, slightly bend your knees. Landing on the balls of your feet (those pads under your toes) also cushions the impact. Feet together? Back straight? Smiling? That's a proper jump.

A slight crouch (page 32) prior to a jump adds height to the jump.

Toe-Touch Jump in Eight Counts

Here's how an eight-count toe-touch jump looks on paper. (Don't try this without your coach's permission! It's an advanced jump that requires flexibility and strength.) Make every movement sharp and crisp. Keep your smiling face looking ahead throughout the jump.

Clean position. Ready, six, seven, eight…
Count 1:
Whip arms into a high V. No arching your back.
Count 2:
Stand on tiptoes, holding your upper body position.
Count 3:
Swing arms down and cross them in a low X as you bend your knees.
Count 4:
Snap your arms up and pull into a T position as you leap up. Tuck your hips under your body while kicking your legs out straight. Point your toes to the ceiling. With a fist or blade hand position, reach for your ankles or calves.
Counts 5 and 6:
Close your legs and land with bent knees, hands still in position at your knees. Feet together, head up, and one big smile!
Count 7:
Return to the clean position.
Count 8:
Hold and smile.

Jump-start Your Jumps

Certain exercises build strength, endurance, and awesome jump height. Quickly repeating the same jump over and over (always with good form) trains your leg muscles to supercharge their upward push. Lunges in sets of ten for each leg also condition jumping muscles.

Your abs need workouts, too. You tighten your abs when you pull yourself into the air—tighter, stronger abs deliver more lifting power.

Ask your coach for help choosing the right exercises for your body.

Learn to love sit-ups.

Every team focuses on fine-tuning different jumps. Don't try any jump before your coach teaches it to you. Without the right technique, it's easy to land wrong and twist your ankle—or worse. Practice your jumps until you have a straight back, good height, a smooth landing, and a big smile every time.

Tuck

Beginners start with tuck jumps, but all cheerleaders do them. Jump straight up, swinging your arms up into a high V. Keep your feet together as you lift your knees up to your chest.

Herkie / Side Hurdler

The herkie jump honors Lawrence Herkimer, one of cheerleading's leaders. He started the first cheerleading company and the first cheerleading camp in the 1940s. In the air, kick one leg out straight to the side and parallel to the ground. Bend the other leg and point the knee to the ground (some teams point their knees forward instead).

The herkie is a popular cheerleading jump.

A squad performs a toe-touch jump.

Spread Eagle

The spread eagle is a showy jump. In the air, snap your arms
to a high V and spread your legs wide apart. Then snap back
for the landing.

For Snappy Toe-Touches:

Lie on the floor, stretching your arms above
your head. Keep your legs straight and
together. Snap them up into a toe-touch
position, working your abs to lift your arms
and hands into position. Quickly snap back
to the starting position. Do sets of five,
working up to twenty snaps.

Chapter 5

Crowds love daring stunts and **pyramids**—two or more stunts linked by the top-row cheerleaders holding each other's hands or legs. School safety rules limit many of these types of advanced moves.

A good coach waits to introduce stunts until the team is ready. Then the coach builds each stunt from its three main parts:

Part 1. Load
The cheerleaders reach stable positions and lift or toss their teammate.

Most schools limit pyramids to two people high.

Part 2. Stunt

The airborne teammate poses or performs, balanced by the supporting teammates.

Part 3. Dismount

The airborne teammate returns to the ground in an upright and pain-free position.

The coach decides how the team will complete each of these parts. You will probably practice just one part over and over (and then again many times) before adding the next move.

Hit the Stunt, Not the Floor

The coach assigns one of three roles to each cheerleader in a stunt: flyer, base, or spotter. These roles may change for every stunt. Coaches might mix assignments so all team members try each role at least once. That way, everyone understands all of the team duties. It also builds trust. If you're a flyer, you must trust your base to catch you. If you're a base or spotter, you must trust your flyer not to crash down on you.

The Base / Lifter / Catcher

As a base, you help lift, hold, and toss the flyer. The flyer stands on the base's thighs, shoulders, or hands. Often, you'll stand very close to another base.

You must be strong and steady. Stand tall with your feet shoulder-width apart and your pelvis tucked in. An arched back is like a bent nail: it can't hold much. Arching also strains your lower back.

When you toss a flyer, you'll likely dip or "sink" with the other bases. The dip is the same springing movement you use in a jump, but it's timed so that all bases dip and release together. Usually, the leader yells, "1-2-Go!" Use your quadriceps to explode upward and launch the flyer.

Base cheerleaders act as lifters and catchers.

41

A flyer catches big air.

Always watch the flyer's hips. They point where the flyer's body will go. The base catches the flyer at the hips, too.

The Flyer / Mounter / Climber

The flyer delivers the razzle-dazzle for the crowds. If you're the flyer, you climb, or mount, the bases to perform an **aerial** pose, jump, or gymnastics move. Keep your body tight when you reach the top of your bases. Your back and legs stay stick-straight. Slouching wobbles your center of gravity.

Let your bases balance for you. Look ahead to help them out. Looking *down* causes you to fall *down*.

Keep your feet at shoulder-width and arms above you or clenched to your sides. Flailing is failing—and dangerous to your bases.

If the bases are supposed to toss you, listen for their countdown. On cue, use your own momentum to add speed, grace, and height to the stunt. Stay in control all the way up into the stunt and back down.

The Third / Scoop / Spotter

A stunt often has one flyer and two or more bases. If you're the "third," you cover the back area and call the counts. The third often works as a base and a spotter. Additional spotters may help with the stunt, even for advanced teams.

Spotters have a huge responsibility to prevent injuries. If you're the spotter, you must know every beat of the routine and dial in on the weakest parts. Pay complete attention. You must react quickly to save the stunt when somebody bobbles.

Stay ready to catch the flyer.

Some coaches prefer spotters to keep their hands up; others like the hands down. Either way, focus on the flyer's head and try to keep your hands on the flyer's foot, ankle, or waist.

Anchor your feet at shoulder-width. If the flyer or anyone else falls, don't flinch. Don't close your eyes. Snag the flyer at the highest point to slow the fall. Always protect the head and neck first.

Catch the flyer. Period.

Because of their strength, guys often serve as spotters— especially for risky three-high college stunts.

43

Thigh Stand Stunt

The thigh stand is good for starter stunters. The bases stand with feet apart and knees bent. A spotter stands behind the bases. A flyers steps onto the bases' thighs. Most often, the flyer strikes a stag or high V position. Since the flyer is close to the ground, falling has a small fear factor. The stunt finishes with a simple step-down dismount.

What Goes Up Must Come Down

Smooth dismounts put the finishing touch on dazzling stunts. The cradle dismount is a crowd favorite. Normally for a cradle, three bases catch the flyer. The back base calls a countdown before the bases dip and pop the flyer slightly into the air. Instantly, the two main catchers grab each other's arms to form a cradle. The flyer drops in a seated position into their arms. The back base watches the flyer's head and shoulders. Then the flyer hops to the floor for the final pose.

The toss dismount follows the same plan, but the bases toss the flyer high into the air. Often, the flyer then performs a spread eagle or some other flashy move before the bases make their catch. Only experienced cheerleaders should try the toss.

From load to dismount, safety rules. Never try a stunt unless your coach agrees that you're ready for it.

Further Reading

Cheerleading in Action by John Crossingham.
    Crabtree Publishing Company, New York, New York, 2003.

Let's Go Team: Cheer, Dance, March / Chants, Cheers, Jumps
    by Craig Peters. Mason Crest Publishers, Philadelphia, 2003.

The Ultimate Guide to Cheerleading by Leslie Wilson.
    Three Rivers Press, New York, New York, 2003.

Web Sites

American Association of Cheerleading Coaches and Advisors
http://www.aacca.org/

CheerHome.com, an online information
clearinghouse
http://www.CheerHome.com/

Ms. Pineapple's Cheer Page
http://www.mspineapple.com/

National Cheerleaders Association
http://www.nationalspirit.com/

National Council for Spirit Safety &
Education
http://www.spiritsafety.com/

United Performing Association, Inc.
http://www.upainc.net/

Universal Cheerleaders Association
http://www.varsity.com

Stick Super (& Safe) Stunts

- Think safety first.
- Trust your teammates.
- Know every part of the stunt.
- Make tight, crisp moves with good form.
- Stay stable and stay up.
- Focus on the stunt and ignore all distractions.
- Listen. Only the person calling the stunt talks.
- Keep a positive attitude.
- Smile!

Glossary

abs (ABZ) — slang for abdomen or stomach muscles

aerial (AIR ee ul) — in the air or overhead

diaphragm (DY uh FRAM) — a plunger-like muscle under the lungs that pulls air into the lungs

endurance (en DOOR uns) — power or strength to keep going or continue for a long time or distance

enthusiasm (en THOO zee AZ um) — excitement or lively interest

enunciate (ee NUN see AYT) — to clearly pronounce words

gestures (JES churz) — hand or arm movements

momentum (moh MENT um) — force or speed of movement

mucous membrane (MYOO kus   MEM BRAYN) — slime-covered thin tissue inside the body

parallel (PAIR uh LEL) — reaching out in the same line; evenly

paralysis (puh RAL uh sus) — loss of movement

peripheral (puh RIF uh rul) — edges, far sides

pompon (POM pon) — in cheerleading, the tufted accessory used to add movement, color, and sound to performances; some dictionaries also use pompom or pom-pom

projection (pruh JEK shun) — in cheerleading, the face expressions, voice, and body posture and gestures that send messages to the audience

pyramids (PIR uh MIDZ) — in cheerleading, several stunts connected by the top-level, or flyer, cheerleaders

vibration (vy BRAY shun) — a fast back-and-forth or quivering movement

Index

About The Author

Tracy Nelson Maurer specializes in nonfiction and business writing. Her most recently published children's books include the *Roaring Rides* series, also from Rourke Publishing LLC. Tracy lives near Minneapolis, Minnesota with her husband Mike and their two children.